BEAVERS

NORTH AMERICAN ANIMAL DISCOVERY LIBRARY

Lynn M. Stone

Rourke Corporation, Inc.
Vero Beach, Florida 32964

PHOTO CREDITS

All photos © Tom and Pat Leeson except: pages 7, 10, 15
© Lynn M. Stone

LIBRARY OF CONGRESS
Library of Congress Cataloging-in-Publication Data
Stone, Lynn M., 1942-
  Beavers / by Lynn M. Stone.

    p. cm. — (North American animal discovery library)
    Summary: An introduction to the physical characteristics,
habits, natural environment, and future prospects of the
beaver.
    ISBN 0-86593-041-4
    1. Beavers—Juvenile literature. [1. Beavers.] I. Title.
II. Series: Stone, Lynn M., 1942- North American animal
discovery library.
QL737.R632S76   1990
599.32'32—dc20   89-70171
                                       CIP
                                       AC

THE BEAVER

You don't need a bulldozer to build a dam. If you are a beaver *(Castor canadensis)*, you can do the job yourself.

Beavers are nature's dam builders. They cut trees and plaster them with mud to build their dams.

The dam backs a stream up and turns what had been dry ground into a pond.

The pond gives the beavers protection. They can disappear by diving or by swimming to the underwater entry to their **lodge.**

Beaver on beaver path

THE BEAVER'S COUSINS

Beavers belong to a family of mammals called **rodents.** Rodents are four-legged, furry animals that gnaw, or chew.

Rodents have two pair of long, sharp teeth known as **incisors.** They have a gap, like a jack-o'-lantern, between their front teeth and back teeth.

Other rodents are the beaver's cousins. Some of them are the tree-climbing squirrels, ground squirrels (like prairie dogs), mice, rats, porcupines, muskrats, woodchucks, and marmots. The beaver is the largest North American rodent north of Panama.

Marmot

TABLE OF CONTENTS

HOW THEY LOOK

Beavers have thick, dark brown fur. Their flat tails are scaly and blackish. Their big front teeth are light brown.

The hind feet of beavers are webbed. The webbing between the beaver's toes helps the beaver paddle in water.

Beavers have small ears and small, dark eyes. The eyes have clear lids that protect them under water.

Beavers don't usually top 60 pounds, but one was weighed at 109 pounds.

Beavers are between 35 and 46 inches in length.

Beaver cutting aspen

WHERE THEY LIVE

An animal's **range** is the entire area in which it might be found. Beavers live throughout most of the United States and Canada. Although some beavers live in the frozen North, others live in northern Florida.

Within their range, beavers have a **habitat.** That is the special type of place where they like to build homes. Beaver habitat includes marshes, rivers, lakes, streams, and ponds.

Beavers that live along rivers do not build dams. They have burrows with underwater entrances in the river bank.

Beaver lodge in Maine

Beaver eating leaves

HOW THEY LIVE

Beaver dams are not watertight. Beavers have to keep cutting trees and repairing their dams.

Beavers are busiest at night. They rarely cut trees or work on their dams in daylight. Because they are slow on land, it is safer for them to cut trees at night.

Beavers weave the trees they cut into their dams and lodges. The mud that they plaster into the branches helps hold water.

Beavers build lodges with a hollow area near the top. A beaver swims into this dry area—a beaver's "living room"—from underwater.

Beaver-cut tree

THE BEAVER'S KITS

A pair of adult beavers probably mate for life. Their babies, called **kits,** are born in May or June.

A mother beaver has from one to eight kits. Most often she has four or five. They can swim less than an hour after birth.

Young beavers stay in their parents' lodge for about 2 years.

Beavers usually live 8 to 10 years. At least one beaver, however, reached 19 years.

Beaver leaving pond

PREDATOR AND PREY

Beavers are plant eaters, or **herbivores.**

Northern beavers eat the leaves and bark of poplar, aspen, willow, and maple trees.

Beavers store twigs and branches in their lodge for winter food.

Sometimes beavers are attacked by meat-eating animals called **predators.** Usually, predators attack young beavers.

Beavers generally are safe when they are in their ponds or lodges. On land they may be **prey,** or food, for coyotes, foxes, bobcats, mountain lions, owls, and hawks.

Beaver gathering winter food

BEAVERS AND PEOPLE

Beaver fur is valuable. In some parts of the beaver's range, people catch beavers in steel leg traps. The beaver's fur is used for clothing and trim on clothing. In other parts of the beaver's range, the beaver is protected from trapping.

During the 1800s, beaver trapping was a big business. Beaver hats and coats were in demand. Trappers visited parts of North America that had never been explored just to find more beavers.

Hundreds of pioneers headed west after hearing the trappers' tales.

Beaver gnawing aspen

THE BEAVER'S FUTURE

Beaver trapping in the 1800s made beavers rare in much of their range. The beaver disappeared completely from many places.

Beavers have some protection from U.S. and Canadian laws now. Beavers again live throughout much of their old range.

Beavers have even become pests to some people. Their dams can flood roads and farm crops. And beavers are not careful about whose trees they chop down.

Most people, however, like having beavers around. Their ponds make good habitat for many animals.

Glossary

habitat (HAB a tat)—the kind of place in which an animal lives, such as a marshland

herbivore (ERB a vore)—an animal that eats plants

incisor (in SI zer)—front teeth made for cutting, in mammals

kit (KIT)—a baby beaver

lodge (LAHDJ)—the dome-shaped house made by a beaver or muskrat

predator (PRED a tor)—an animal that kills other animals for food

prey (PRAY)—an animal that is hunted by another for food

range (RAYNJ)—the entire area in which a certain type of animal lives

rodent (RO dent)—a large group of mammals that gnaw

INDEX